CINDERELLA

AND THE

QUEST

FOR THE

CRYSTAL PUMP

BY
L. HENRY DOWELL

BLACK BOX THEATRE PUBLISHING

ISBN 978-0615542140

Printed in the United States of America.

CAST

Touchstone
Prince Charming
The King
The Queen
Magic Mirror
Cinderella
Stepmother
Brumhilda
Grizelda
Cryer
Fairy Godperson
Dr. Thingamabob
Clockwork Cindy
Colonel Klamauk
Klink
Klank
Master Fuzzy
Fuzzy Forest Ninjas
Snow White
Little Dwarf #1
Little Dwarf #2
Sleeping Beauty
Pocahontas
The Little Mermaid
Rapunzel
Old Professor
Spiders

Cinderella and the Quest for the Crystal Pump

SCENE ONE

LIGHTS: RISE to reveal a beautiful palace. MUSIC:
Classical style fairy tale music plays.
TOUCHSTONE THE JESTER enters looking
around.

TOUCHSTONE

Yoo hoo! Prince Charming? Where are you? Your Majesty?
(Notices audience.)
Oh, hello there. Listen. Have you seen the Prince anywhere?
His parents are looking for him…again! My goodness, that
boy is always running off!
(Resumes looking.)
Prince Charming?

PRINCE enters, more zero than hero.

PRINCE

What is it, Touchstone?

TOUCHSTONE

There you are! Where have you been? The King and Queen
have been looking all over the place for you! Don't you know
what today is?

PRINCE

Yes, I am well aware of what today is.

TOUCHSTONE

(Looking off into the distance.)
Oh dear! Here come your parents!

MUSIC: Trumpet flourish as KING and
QUEEN enter.

KING
Prince Charming! We have been looking all over for you!

PRINCE
So I heard.

QUEEN
Don't you know what today is?

PRINCE
Yes mother. I know all too well what today is. My birthday

QUEEN
That's right. Your birthday!

> TOUCHSTONE blows a whirly gig. ALL
> shoot HIM a look.

TOUCHSTONE
Sorry.

KING
Where have you been, my son? Out slaying a dragon maybe?

QUEEN
Or rescuing a damsel in distress perhaps?

TOUCHSTONE
Or maybe fighting off an evil horde!

PRINCE
I was reading.

KING
Reading?

QUEEN
Reading?

TOUCHSTONE

Reading?

PRINCE

That's right. I was reading. I just wanted to find a nice quiet little corner of the castle where no one would bother me and enjoy a good book. Surely, that isn't a bad thing?

KING

Certainly not. Reading is a fine thing. Many people read. In fact, I do it on occasion myself.

TOUCHSTONE

You do?

KING
(Shoots TOUCHSTONE another look.)
Of course I do.

QUEEN

As do I. We were just hoping that maybe you were out doing something....I don't know....something...

TOUCHSTONE

Less wimpy?

KING
(Another look.)
More "princely". You are to be the ruler of this kingdom some day, and the people must be able to look up to you, my son. Your grandfather was a great dragon slayer. Everybody looked up to him. The tales of his greatness were made into songs. And my father, well, there was no finer horseman in all the land.

QUEEN

And your father, Prince Charming...he risked life and limb to rescue me from an evil witch, deep within the Black Forest.

8

KING
Please dear!

QUEEN
You are too modest, my darling.

KING
No. I meant please, go on.

QUEEN
He was just a young prince then. Dashing and brave. And he won my heart that day.

The KING and QUEEN nuzzle.

PRINCE AND TOUCHSTONE
Eeeeewwwww, old people love!

KING
But today is your day my son. It's your…

PRINCE
Birthday. Yes, we've established that already.

QUEEN
Your father and I wanted to give you your gift as soon as you awoke, but we couldn't find you.

PRINCE
Here I am now.

KING
Indeed you are. Touchstone!

TOUCHSTONE
(Coming to attention and saluting.)
Yes, your Majesty?

KING

Go get the gift!

TOUCHSTONE

Yes, Sir! As you command! Right away, Sir!
            (But HE doesn't move. The KING shoots HIM
            another look.)
Oh…right!

HE exits running.

KING

I think you are going to be most surprised with this gift. It's
something very special.

PRINCE

Is it that new set of encyclopedias I asked for?

KING

No...wait, how are encyclopedias something very special?

PRINCE

They're special to me.

TOUCHSTONE enters pushing large
wrapped object.

TOUCHSTONE

Before he opens his gift, shouldn't we sing a certain song?

QUEEN

An excellent idea Touchstone.

TOUCHSTONE
            (To audience.)
Will you help us sing for Prince Charles Edward Tiberius
Charming III? You will? Fantastic!

EVERYONE

Happy Birthday to you! Happy Birthday to you! Happy
Birthday Prince Charles Edward Tiberius Charming III!
Happy Birthday to you!

QUEEN

Now open your gift!

> PRINCE starts to tear open wrapping paper
> to reveal the head of the MAGIC MIRROR.

MIRROR

Here's Johnny!

PRINCE

Wow. It's furniture. That talks. And does Jack Nicholson
impressions!

KING

It's a mirror!

QUEEN

It's a magic mirror!

PRINCE
(Sarcastically.)
Just what I've always wanted.

QUEEN

We found it at a garage sale!

PRINCE

Went all out, huh?

KING

Evidently, it has quite a bit of history attached to it. It once
belonged to an evil queen.

PRINCE
This just keeps getting better.

QUEEN
The queen would use its magic for all sorts of purposes, dark and sinister.

KING
You'll find this mirror to be quite articulate.

QUEEN
And very well read.

MIRROR
That's me!

QUEEN
And extremely intelligent. Watch this. Magic Mirror on the wall, who's the fairest one of all?

MIRROR
(To the audience.)
I ain't no dummy!
(To the QUEEN.)
You O'Queen are the fairest in the land!

QUEEN
Oooooo, I just love this thing!

PRINCE
You keep it then.

QUEEN
No. It's your gift. Besides, I have your father to tell me how beautiful I am.

KING
It's true. You are a very lovely woman.

THEY nuzzle again.

PRINCE AND TOUCHSTONE
Eeeeewwwww, old people love!

QUEEN
It says other things too! Watch this. Magic Mirror on the
wall, should we throw the Prince a masquerade ball?

MIRROR
As I see it, yes.

KING
Will there be cake at this masquerade ball?

MIRROR
Most likely.

QUEEN
Is that all you care about? Cake?

MIRROR
It is decidedly so.

THEY look at the MIRROR who just
smiles.

PRINCE
Mother. Father. I thank you for your gift. It is a most unusual
treasure, but the last thing I want is for someone to throw me
ball!

TOUCHSTONE throws a beach ball at
PRINCE. THEY shoot HIM another look.

TOUCHSTONE
What? It's a sight gag. I'm a jester. It's my job.
(THEY stare harder. HE pulls out a banana.)
Wanna see me slip on a banana peel?

ALL
NO!!!

KING
Prince Charming. If you stay cooped up here in the castle all
the time, how in the world will you ever have any
adventures?

PRINCE
Adventures are overrated.

QUEEN
How will you ever meet any girls?

PRINCE
Girls are overrated, too.

THEY look at EACH OTHER.

QUEEN
(Looking at KING.)
But...what about...grandchildren?

PRINCE
Good grief. Not this again.

KING
Son. You aren't getting any younger.

TOUCHSTONE
No doubt about that!
(THEY look at HIM.)
Sorry.

PRINCE

I'm only 38!

KING

And you've never even fought a dragon! Why when I was a young man...

PRINCE

No offense Father, but I'm not you.

QUEEN

Charles Edward Tiberius Charming III!

PRINCE

Charlie.

QUEEN

Excuse me?

PRINCE

We've been over this, Mother. I prefer to be called Charlie.

QUEEN

That's ridiculous. That would make you Charlie Charming. Who ever heard of a Prince named Charlie Charming?

> TOUCHSTONE snickers. THEY shoot HIM another look. HE stops.

TOUCHSTONE

Sorry.

KING

Son. Let us do this. Let us have the ball. It would mean a lot to your Mother. We'll invite every eligible maiden in the kingdom and just see what happens. Ok? You never know. The "right" girl just might show up!

QUEEN

Please...Charlie? For me? You never know. Pleeeeeeeeeease?

PRINCE
(Giving in.)
As you wish, Mother.

> SHE kisses HIM on the head. QUEEN and
> KING exit.

PRINCE
(Turns to MIRROR.)
Mirror...what do you think? Will I ever find the "right" girl?

MIRROR

Reply hazy. Try again later.

PRINCE

That figures.
(To audience.)
Aw gee whiz! What have I gotten myself into now? The "right" girl? What does that mean anyway? No "left" girls? What does the "right" girl look like anyway? Would I know her if I ran into her on the street?
(Pauses, thinking.)
No. I'm not ready for this. I'm afraid of girls. I know! I'll run away!

TOUCHSTONE

You can't! The King and Queen, they're throwing you a masquerade ball! You can't just run away!

PRINCE

Of course I can. Just tell my parents I went out to slay a
dragon…a big red one with all kinds of claws and
teeth…and…oh…I know, tell them I went out to rescue a
damsel in distress…or fight an evil horde…I don't
know…tell them I went out to fight an evil horde of damsels
and rescue a dragon in distress. Either way, I'm sure they'll
be ecstatic. They'll forget all about this masquerade ball
business.

TOUCHSTONE

Prince Charming. Charlie. Old buddy. Old pal. You know I
cannot lie to the King and Queen. Make fun of them, yes.
Fart in their presence, yes. But lie to them…no. I can't.

PRINCE
(Thinking.)
Come with me then.

TOUCHSTONE

What? Out there? In the real world?

PRINCE

Why not?

TOUCHSTONE

But…I'm a jester? I've been a jester my whole life. What
would I do out there?

PRINCE

Who knows? Go in to politics maybe.

TOUCHSTONE

If we go…and we don't like it…can we ever come back?

PRINCE

Not according to Thomas Wolfe.

TOUCHSTONE

Who's that?

PRINCE

Nevermind.

TOUCHSTONE

Ok. I'll do it. Just so I can watch over you.

MIRROR

Hey...guys?

PRINCE

Mirror?

MIRROR

Can I go, too?

PRINCE

You want to come with us?

MIRROR

Sure. It beats hanging around here all the time.
            (Laughs way too long and way too hard.)

PRINCE

Yes. That's a good one. I guess with your ability to tell
fortunes you might come in handy. You tell us. Magic Mirror
on the wall, would it be to our advantage to take you along?

MIRROR

Ask again later.

PRINCE

What?

MIRROR

Better not tell you now!

                    PRINCE
What?

                    MIRROR
Most likely?

              THEY give HER a look.

                    MIRROR
Yes.

                    PRINCE
Good. Now if we are going out into the real world, we are
going to need some disguises.

                    TOUCHSTONE
I have just the thing right here.
              (Pulls mustaches out of pocket.)

                    PRINCE
Fake mustaches?

                    TOUCHSTONE
Yep!

              THEY put them on. MIRROR too.

                    PRINCE
I look like Gene Shalit.

                    TOUCHSTONE
Who?

                    PRINCE
Nevermind. And now, we're off to find a life completely
devoid of adventure and absolutely no girls whatsoever!

ALL
No girls whatsoever!!!

LIGHTS: BLACKOUT.

SCENE TWO

LIGHTS: RISE on Cinderella's cottage. CINDERELLA
enters wearing work clothes. SHE sweeps and
seems happy.

STEPMOTHER
(Offstage.)
Cinderella? Are you finished with that sweeping yet?

CINDERELLA
Not yet, Stepmother!

BRUMHILDA
(Offstage.)
Cinderella? Did you get that laundry done? I can't find my
purple bloomers!

CINDERELLA
Not yet, Brumhilda!

GRIZELDA
(Offstage.)
Cinderella! Don't forget to wash the dishes!

CINDERELLA
Will do, Grizelda!

STEPMOTHER
And feed the fish!

BRUMHILDA
And milk the cow!

GRIZELDA
And mow the grass!

STEPMOTHER
And beat the rugs!

BRUMHILDA
And take out the trash!

GRIZELDA
And churn the buttermilk!

ALL
CINDERELLA!!!

CINDERELLA
Yes! I heard you! I'll get everything done I promise.
(To audience.)
Gee whiz! My life is so bland and boring! I just can't stand it
sometimes! "Cinderella, do the dishes!" "Cinderella, beat the
rugs!" "Cinderella, fold the laundry!" "Cinderella, churn the
buttermilk!" I hate buttermilk! Am I crazy for wanting to
know what's out…there? Beyond these walls?

STEPMOTHER enters.

STEPMOTHER
Cinderella. Come here and sit beside me.
(THEY sit.)
I know you have a lot of work to do.

CINDERELLA
Yes ma'am! I certainly do.
STEPMOTHER
Things have been very difficult ever since your beloved
father disappeared.

CINDERELLA
I know.

STEPMOTHER

I want to do something to help you get all of your chores done.

CINDERELLA

That would be wonderful! Thank you so much!

STEPMOTHER

I want to give you some...advice.

CINDERELLA

Advice?

STEPMOTHER

You must learn to manage your time better, my dear. Multi-task. Learn to do two things at once. Like beating the rugs <u>and</u> churning the buttermilk at the same time. You do have two hands you know. Do you understand me, Cinderella?

CINDERELLA

I think so.

STEPMOTHER

Good. I'm so glad we had this little talk. Now get back to work!
       (CINDERELLA resumes cleaning.
       STEPMOTHER addresses audience.)
Have you ever noticed the bias in these stories against stepmothers? I just want to go on the record here as being against this sort of negative stereotyping. Stepmothers have a very difficult job you know. Blending two separate families together into one cohesive unit is tough enough, and when you factor in the mysterious disappearance of my husband, Henry. He was a famous explorer you know. Well, that sort of thing is apt to make any woman...grouchy. You know what I mean? It's not that I dislike Cinderella...

CINDERELLA
Stepmother, would you...

STEPMOTHER
(Yelling.)
In a minute Cinderella! Can't you see I'm doing my
monologue!

CINDERELLA
Sorry.

STEPMOTHER
Where was I? Oh yes. It's not that I really dislike Cinderella.
She just...I don't know...annoys the living crap out of me
with all her sweetness! All her "pleases" and "thank yous"
and "yes Ma'ams". I bet she was an honor roll student too.

CINDERELLA
I was.
(STEPMOTHER shoots HER a look.)
Sorry.

STEPMOTHER
Anyway...my point is, that it's a very difficult job and people
shouldn't be so quick to judge us stepmothers, at least not till
you've walked a mile in my expensive and highly
fashionable footwear.

SOUND: Doorbell rings. BRUMHILDA
enters.

BRUMHILDA
Someone's at the door.

SOUND: Doorbell rings. GRIZELDA
enters.

GRIZELDA
Anybody going to get the door?

SOUND: Doorbell rings. THEY look at
CINDERELLA.

CINDERELLA
I'll get the door.

SHE exits, then re-enters with CRYER.

CRYER
By order of the Royal Family...a masquerade ball will be
held Saturday next in celebration of the birthday of Prince
Charles Edward Tiberius Charming III! All eligible maidens
living in the kingdom are hereby invited to attend.

STEPMOTHER
A ball?

BRUMHILDA
A ball?

GRIZELDA
A ball?

CRYER
A masquerade ball, to be precise.

STEPMOTHER
Anything in that notice about an age limit?

CRYER
No...but there should have been.

CRYER exits.

STEPMOTHER

Snit.
            (To GIRLS.)
Hot dog! We're going to the big dance, girls!

BRUMHILDA

Excuse me?

GRIZELDA

Did you just say "we"?

STEPMOTHER

That's right. "We". Maybe the Prince's taste in women runs
to the ever so slightly more mature.

BRUMHILDA AND GRIZELDA

Bwah-ha-ha-ha-ha!

            STEPMOTHER shoots THEM a look.
            THEY shut up.

BRUMHILDA AND GRIZELDA

Sorry.

STEPMOTHER

Let's face it. When you've got it, you've got it.

BRUMHILDA

I'm going to look gorgeous! There's no way the Prince will
be able to resist me!

GRIZELDA

Are you kidding? He'll take one look at me and forget your
name!

BRUMHILDA

He's mine! You hear me?

GRIZELDA

Over my dead body!

BRUMHILDA

That can be arranged you know!

GRIZELDA

Mother! Brumhilda just threatened me!

STEPMOTHER

I don't care. Just don't get any blood on the floor. Cinderella is far too busy to clean it up.

(CINDERELLA nods in agreement.)

Oh girls! There's so much to do! We have to find dresses and get our hair done.

CINDERELLA

Stepmother?

STEPMOTHER

Yes, Cinderella? What is it?

CINDERELLA

May I go to the masquerade ball, too?

STEPMOTHER

Excuse me?

CINDERELLA

I never get to go anywhere. It would only be for one night.

BRUMHILDA

Poor Cinderella!

GRIZELDA

She seems to think she'd have a chance at nabbing the Prince for herself!

ALL

Bwah-ha-ha-ha-ha!

STEPMOTHER

Is that true Cinderella? Do you think the Prince might fancy a girl as plain and ordinary as yourself?

CINDERELLA

Oh no. Of course not. It's not that at all. I would just like to get out of here for a while.

STEPMOTHER

Well, I suppose you could go, provided you can find a suitable dress. I will not have you embarrassing us by showing up at the Royal Palace in rags!

CINDERELLA

Of course not.

STEPMOTHER

You'll have to get all of your chores done first.

CINDERELLA

Yes, Ma'am.

STEPMOTHER

Very well. Come girls! We must go shopping!

BRUMHILDA AND GRIZELDA

Shopping!

THEY exit. CINDERELLA turns to the audience.

CINDERELLA

I just want to get out of here. See the world beyond these four walls. I want to travel and meet people. All kinds of people. I want to have adventures! <u>I want to go to that ball!</u> Is that too much to wish for?

>THE FAIRY GODPERSON appears in a puff of smoke and music.

FAIRY GODPERSON

Why, no my dear. Not too much at all.

CINDERELLA

Who are you...and how did you get in here?

FAIRY GODPERSON

I am your Fairy Godperson. I go where I wish.

CINDERELLA

Fairy God "person"?

FAIRY GODPERSON

It's the world we live in my dear. Even the fairy tales are getting all politically correct.

CINDERELLA

Why are you here?

FAIRY GODPERSON

I am here to grant your fondest wish.

CINDERELLA

Really?

FAIRY GODPERSON

Hey, would I lie?

CINDERELLA
I don't know. I just met you.

FAIRY GODPERSON
Oh, I'm very honest. Take my word for it.

CINDERELLA
And you are here to grant my fondest wish?

FAIRY GODPERSON
Indeed. I'm a Fairy Godperson, it's what I do.

CINDERELLA
That's fantastic!

FAIRY GODPERSON
I thought you'd like that...and just what is your fondest wish
Cinderella?

CINDERELLA
I wish to go to the ball!

FAIRY GODPERSON
The Prince's masquerade ball?

CINDERELLA
That's the one.

FAIRY GODPERSON
I see. You'll need a dress.

CINDERELLA
Of course.

FAIRY GODPERSON
A fabulous dress.

CINDERELLA

Please!

FAIRY GODPERSON

And we have to do something about your hair!

CINDERELLA

I figured.

FAIRY GODPERSON

And shoes!

CINDERELLA

Shoes?

FAIRY GODPERSON

You'll need some new shoes!

CINDERELLA

I do love new shoes!

FAIRY GODPERSON

Who doesn't? And we are not talking about any old shoes!

CINDERELLA

Oh no?

FAIRY GODPERSON

Oh no! For this you'll need the perfect shoes to accentuate
that cute little footsie of yours! A pair of shoes befitting a
princess!

CINDERELLA

A princess?

FAIRY GODPERSON

Indeed! For this you will require nothing less than the perfect
pair of Crystal Pumps!

CINDERELLA

Oh my!!!

FAIRY GODPERSON

You will have to earn these things, Cinderella!

CINDERELLA

But how?

FAIRY GODPERSON

You must go on a quest! But it won't be easy!

CINDERELLA

My father used to say that "nothing worth having ever is".
Easy that is.

FAIRY GODPERSON

Your father sounds like a wise man.

CINDERELLA

He is. Was. He was a famous explorer. He disappeared
mysteriously some years ago.

FAIRY GODPERSON

Do not trouble yourself with such things right now,
Cinderella. Keep your mind on the task at hand. It will be a
grand adventure indeed, Cinderella!

CINDERELLA

But what about my stepmother? Won't she miss me? She'll
never agree to let me go to the ball once she learns I've run
away on this "grand adventure".

FAIRY GODPERSON

Hmmmm. I hadn't thought of that. I have an idea though.

HE pulls out a cell phone.

CINDERELLA

What's that?

FAIRY GODPERSON

This is called a cell phone. They'll be very big one day. I'm sending, what's called, a text.

CINDERELLA

Text?

FAIRY GODPERSON

OMG. Its a message of sorts. I'm contacting an associate of mine who might be able to help in this matter.

SOUND: Doorbell.

FAIRY GODPERSON

That'll be him!

CINDERELLA

That was fast.

FAIRY GODPERSON

Cinderella, may I introduce Dr. Thaddeus Thingamabob!

DR. THINGAMABOB enters. HE is an elf inventor.

CINDERELLA

How do you do, Dr. Thingamajig?

DR. THINGAMABOB

Thingamabob. And I do very well. How do you do?

CINDERELLA

Very well thank you.

FAIRY GODPERSON
Dr. Thingamabob is an award winning elf inventor.

CINDERELLA
Oh really?

DR. THINGAMABOB
Yes. Two silvers and a bronze.

Silence.

FAIRY GODPERSON
(To CINDERELLA.)
That was his attempt at humor.

CINDERELLA
Oh…ha-ha-ha-ha….so, you say he's an elf?

FAIRY GODPERSON
Yes. You'll note his pointy ears.

CINDERELLA
And just how is Dr. Thingamahooey going to help me?

DR. THINGAMABOB
Thingamabob. And I am going to replace you.

CINDERELLA
Excuse me?

FAIRY GODPERSON
Only temporarily, my dear. You will need someone to take
your place while you are away.

CINDERELLA
Who could possibly do that?

DR. THINGAMABOB
Allow me to introduce my latest invention…

HE pulls out a remote control. Twists some
knobs. CLOCKWORK CINDY enters. SHE
is a robot version of CINDERELLA.

DR. THINGAMABOB
I call her the Cinderella 3000…or Clockwork Cindy for
short!

CINDERELLA
Clockwork Cindy?

FAIRY GODPERSON
She'll be the perfect stand in for you. No one will suspect a
thing.

CINDERELLA
Can she talk?

FAIRY GODPERSON
Can she talk? What a question! Can she talk! Ha….she can
talk, can't she, Doctor?

DR. THINGAMABOB
Of course!

HE flips some switches.

CLOCKWORK CINDY
Ho-Ho-Ho!

THEY give DR. THINGAMABOB a look.

DR. THINGAMABOB
Sorry.

HE makes an adjustment to CLOCKWORK
CINDY, and then pushes a button.

CLOCKWORK CINDY

I love to clean.
(Pause.)
I love to bake.
(Pause.)
Oooo, is that a new broom?

CINDERELLA

I don't sound like that.

FAIRY GODPERSON

Sure you do. Don't worry about a thing, Cinderella. Dr.
Thingamabob here is a pro. He used to work at the North
Pole.

CINDERELLA

Really? What happened?

DR. THINGAMABOB

Uh…it was too cold. Brrrrrr.

CINDERELLA

Ok. I guess I'm on my way then. Wish me luck!

FAIRY GODPERSON

And don't forget, you have to be back home by midnight!

CINDERELLA

Why midnight?

FAIRY GODPERSON

This is Children's Theatre honey. If these little kids have to
sit here for more than ninety minutes they'll pee in their
seats, and we don't want that.

CINDERELLA
No. Nobody wants that!

FAIRY GODPERSON
Oh, and before I forget, here is a map to aid you on your
quest.
(HE hands HER a map.)

CINDERELLA
Thank you! Goodbye!

FAIRY GODPERSON
Goodbye and good luck, my dear!

CINDERELLA exits, waving.

DR. THINGAMABOB
She's going to need it.

FAIRY GODPERSON
No doubt.

CLOCKWORK CINDY
Ho-Ho-Ho.

LIGHTS: BLACKOUT.

SCENE THREE

LIGHTS: RISE on a street scene. CINDERELLA enters on
            one side reading a map. PRINCE enters on the
            other side reading a map, followed by MIRROR,
            and TOUCHSTONE. PRINCE and CINDERELLA
            run into EACH OTHER.

PRINCE AND CINDERELLA
Sorry!

PRINCE
It was my fault. I'm such a klutz.

CINDERELLA
No. I should watch where I'm going.

PRINCE
Where were you going?

CINDERELLA
Pardon?

PRINCE
My friends and I are kind of lost.

CINDERELLA
Me too, I'm afraid. I'm sorry, I didn't catch your name?

PRINCE
It's…Charlie. My name is Charlie.
            (To MIRROR.)
This is my friend…Mario.

MIRROR
Hiya!

PRINCE
(To TOUCHSTONE.)
And this is his brother…Luigi.

TOUCHSTONE

Lets a go!

CINDERELLA
Those are very interesting names.

TOUCHSTONE
Don't blame us. We didn't pick 'em.

TOUCHSTONE and MIRROR give
PRINCE a dirty look.

CINDERELLA
My name's Cinderella. I'm very pleased to meet all of you.

PRINCE
The pleasure is all ours. Listen, my friends and I, we're not
from around here. Do you think that maybe we could tag
along with you for a while?

CINDERELLA
I don't know. I'm kind of on a quest.

PRINCE
A quest? Really? For what?

CINDERELLA
Shoes…I guess you could say.

PRINCE

Shoes?
                    (To HIMSELF.)
That sounds pretty boring!
                    (To CINDERELLA.)
We'd love to come along with you on your quest for shoes, if
it's ok with you, Cinderella.

CINDERELLA

I suppose it would be all right. I'm searching for the perfect
pair of Crystal Pumps.

PRINCE

Sounds fancy.

CINDERELLA

I'm going to the Prince's masquerade ball. I want to look my
best.

PRINCE

The Prince's masquerade ball? Oh…that sounds like great
fun.

CINDERELLA

I hope so. Every maiden in the kingdom will be there.

PRINCE

Probably. I hear the Prince's mother and father really want
him to get married.

TOUCHSTONE

And have grandchildren!
                    (PRINCE shoots HIM a dirty look.)
Sorry.

CINDERELLA

I wonder what the Prince is really like. He's probably a total
jerk.

TOUCHSTONE and MIRROR snicker.

PRINCE
I hear he's a pretty nice guy. Isn't that right…Mario? Luigi?

MIRROR
Whatever you say, boss.

TOUCHSTONE
Let's a go!

CINDERELLA
I have no idea what I'd even say to the Prince if I did meet him. "What's shaking, Prince?" "How 'bout them Mets?"

PRINCE
Maybe you could just start out with "Hi. My name is Cinderella. Pleased to meet you."

CINDERELLA
Yeah. That might work. I'll remember that if it ever happens, which right now is very doubtful.

TOUCHSTONE
Oh, I don't know. I'd say the odds are better than you think.

CINDERELLA
You think so?

MIRROR
You may rely on it.

PRINCE
So, where are these Crystal Pumps that you're looking for?

CINDERELLA
According to this map, it's over the river and across the green.

PRINCE

Kind of a funny place for a shoe store, but what are we waiting on?

(To MIRROR and TOUCHSTONE.)

Guys?

MIRROR AND TOUCHSTONE

Let's a go!

THEY join hands and skip off.
COLONEL KLAMAUK, KLINK, and
KLANK enter.

COLONEL KLAMAUK

Klink! Klank! Hast du gehort was ich gehort haben? (Klink! Klank! Did you hear what I heard?)

KLINK and KLANK

Ja, Colonel Klamauk! (Yes, Colonel Klamauk!)

COLONEL KLAMAUK

Sie sind auf deinem Crystal Pumps suchen! (They are looking for the Crystal Pumps!)

KLINK

Was fur ein Zufall! (What a coincidence!)

KLANK

So sind wir! (So are we!)

COLONEL KLAMAUK

Naturlich dumkopfe! Lasst uns ihnen zu folgen! (Of course dummies! Let's follow them!)

KLINK and KLANK

Ja, Colonel Klamauk! (Yes, Colonel Klamauk!)

THEY exit. LIGHTS: BLACKOUT.

SCENE FOUR

LIGHTS: RISE on a forest scene. CINDERELLA, PRINCE,
            MIRROR, and TOUCHSTONE enter slowly,
            looking around.

TOUCHSTONE
Wh…where are we?

CINDERELLA
According to this map, we are in the Black Forest.

PRINCE
And just why are we in such a scary place when we are
supposed to be shoe shopping?

TOUCHSTONE
I thought we were going to the mall.

MIRROR
Me too. I wanted a slushy.

CINDERELLA
Evidently there's something here that will show us the way to
the Crystal Pumps.

PRINCE
These better be some awesome shoes!

CINDERELLA
Oh, they are! I know it. They just have to be!

TOUCHSTONE
Look! Someone's coming. Someone really short.

MASTER FUZZY enters.

CINDERELLA
Uh…hi? Could you help us?

MASTER FUZZY
To me talking, you are?

CINDERELLA
Yes. I think. Huh?

MASTER FUZZY
My counsel, seek you?

TOUCHSTONE
Wow! This guy's grammar sucks.

MASTER FUZZY
Heard that, I did!

TOUCHSTONE
Sorry, I am.

CINDERELLA
This map led me here. It was given to me by my Fairy
Godperson. I'm looking for…

MASTER FUZZY
Know I, what you seek. The Cavern of the Crystal Pump.

PRINCE
Cavern? Who puts a shoe store in a cave?

CINDERELLA
            (To PRINCE.)
Shhhh.
            (To MASTER FUZZY.)
Yes. We seek the way and we were hoping that you could
help us…

MASTER FUZZY
Master Fuzzy, my name is, and help you, I will.

ALL
YAY!!!

MASTER FUZZY
After test, you pass.

ALL
SAY WHAT???

MASTER FUZZY
Worthy, you must be. Prove it, you must.

TOUCHSTONE
We're quite worthy I assure you, this guy is…

PRINCE elbows HIM.

PRINCE
…wondering what we might have to do to prove our worth,
Master Fuzzy?

MASTER FUZZY
Battle, you must.

MIRROR
Oh poop!

TOUCHSTONE
I'm a lover! Not a fighter!

PRINCE
You want us to battle?

MASTER FUZZY
Repeat myself, I will not.

CINDERELLA
You really want us to fight to prove ourselves to you?

MASTER FUZZY
Repeat myself, I will not.

TOUCHSTONE
But you just...

PRINCE elbows HIM again.

PRINCE
Ok then. If you want us to battle...we'll battle.

HE grabs TOUCHSTONE and puts HIM in
a headlock. THEY all battle EACH OTHER.

MASTER FUZZY
Morons.
(THEY stop.)
Among yourselves, do not fight.

CINDERELLA
Then who do we battle?

MASTER FUZZY
Them.

FUZZY FOREST NINJAS enter quickly
and take a battle stance.

ALL
Oh poop!

MASTER FUZZY
Ready! Fight!

MUSIC: BATTLE MUSIC. Large fight.
Eventually only CINDERELLA remains.
MASTER FUZZY claps.

MASTER FUZZY
Most impressive, Cinderella.

CINDERELLA
Thank you. Will you help us now?

MASTER FUZZY
I will.

CINDERELLA
How do we get to the Cavern of the Crystal Pump?

MASTER FUZZY
No idea, have I.

CINDERELLA
What? You have no idea?

MASTER FUZZY
Nope.

CINDERELLA
Then, what was all of this for?

MASTER FUZZY
Enjoy a good fight, do I.

CINDERELLA
Thanks for nothing. Let's go guys.

MASTER FUZZY
Wait! Know the way, I do not. Know the way to the one who
knows the way, I do.

TOUCHSTONE
Say what?

MASTER FUZZY
Seek you the one who went before.

CINDERELLA
Who is that? I don't understand.

MASTER FUZZY
Now go. Master Fuzzy other entertainment seeks.

THEY start to exit.

PRINCE
Where are we going, Cinderella?

CINDERELLA
I'm not sure…but evidently, we're going to find out.

THEY exit. THE FUZZY FOREST
CREATURES back off stage. COLONEL
KLAMAUK, KLINK and KLANK enter.

COLONEL KLAMAUK
Sie haben diesen weg gekommen! (They came this way!)

KLINK
Ich bin angstlich! (I'm scared!)

KLANK
Ich auch!   (Me too!)

COLONEL KLAMAUK
Wer ist das klienste Kreatur?   (Who is this little creature?)

KLINK
Er ist sehr fuzzy!   (He is so fuzzy!)

                    KLANK
Und niedlich!   (And cute!)

                    MASTER FUZZY
Into this forest, you should not have come.

                    FUZZY FOREST CREATURES enter
                    quickly.

                    ALL
Oh poop!   (Oh poop!)

                    LIGHTS: BLACKOUT.

SCENE FIVE

LIGHTS: RISE on Snow White's cottage. Similar to
            Cinderella's. CINDERELLA, PRINCE, MIRROR,
            and TOUCHSTONE enter.

CINDERELLA
You guys wait outside. I'll see if anybody's home.

PRINCE
Ok Cinderella. If you say so, but be careful.

CINDERELLA
I will.

SHE knocks.

SNOW WHITE
(From offstage.)
Come on in.

CINDERELLA enters cottage.

CINDERELLA
Hello?

SNOW WHITE enters. Pregnant with hair
up in curlers.

SNOW WHITE
Well hello there!
CINDERELLA
Snow White? Wow! I never thought I'd run into you way out
here in...well...

SNOW WHITE
The boondocks?

CINDERELLA
I wasn't going to say that…but…yes.

SNOW WHITE
It's ok. I like it out here in the middle of nowhere. Very
peaceful.
(SOUND: Baby screams offstage.)
Most of the time. So, what brings you so deep into the black
forest?

CINDERELLA
I'm searching for the Cavern of the Crystal Pump.

SNOW WHITE
The Crystal Pump? That's ironic.

CINDERELLA
Ironic? How so?

SNOW WHITE
There was a gentleman who came through here looking for
the Crystal Pump. It was some time ago however.

CINDERELLA
Very interesting.

SNOW WHITE
May I ask you a question?

CINDERELLA
Of course.

SNOW WHITE
Why do you seek the Crystal Pumps?

CINDERELLA
I want to go to the Prince's ball.

SNOW WHITE
Looking for a "happily ever after"?

CINDERELLA
Maybe.

SNOW WHITE
There's nothing wrong with that. It's what we all look for.
But just remember this... love isn't always found in a big
castle in the arms of a prince. Sometimes it's right in front of
us. Look at me. I fell in love with a dwarf and I couldn't be
happier.

LITTLE DWARF #1 and #2 enter.

LITTLE DWARF #1
Mommy! He hit me!

LITTLE DWARF #2
I did not! She's lying!

LITTLE DWARF #1
I am not! He hit me!

LITTLE DWARF #2
Did not!

LITTLE DWARF #1
Did too!

LITTLE DWARF #2
Did not!

SNOW WHITE
Both of you! Go to your rooms!

LITTLE DWARVES
Yes, Mommy.

THEY run offstage.

CINDERELLA
Happily ever after?

SNOW WHITE
Oh sure. No one ever tells you what that means when you're
a little girl growing up. Diapers. The mortgage. PTA
meetings. Don't get me wrong, Cinderella, I love my life. Six
little dwarves…
    (Pats HER belly.)
…and one on the way. I wouldn't trade places with anybody.

LITTLE DWARVES
    (Offstage.)
Mommy!!!

SNOW WHITE
Don't make me come in there!

Silence.

Other PRINCESSES enter.

SNOW WHITE
Why hello girls! You remember Cinderella?

PRINCESSES
Hello. Yes of course. Good to see you. Etc.

CINDERELLA
Hello girls.

SNOW WHITE
Cinderella is on a quest!

POCAHONTAS
You go, girlfriend!

RAPUNZEL
What are you questing for?

CINDERELLA
The Crystal Pumps.

PRINCESSES
Gasp!

SLEEPING BEAUTY
Wow! When you quest, you don't fool around.

THE LITTLE MERMAID
Is there a man at stake?

POCAHONTAS
A prince maybe?

REPUNZEL
A "charming" prince?

CINDERELLA
Maybe. We'll see.

SLEEPING BEAUTY
(Yawning.)
Believe me Cinderella, we understand. Don't we, girls?

PRINCESSES
You better believe it. That's right. Ain't that the truth? Etc.

CINDERELLA
Mostly I just want to get out of the house. See the world a
little bit.

SNOW WHITE

I remember those feelings. My stepmother used to keep me locked up in the palace cleaning all the time. I couldn't wait to get out and live a little bit.

LITTLE DWARVES

Mommy!!!

SNOW WHITE

I'm counting to three. ONE...
        (Silence.)
We're having a bridge game, if you want to stay and play a hand.

CINDERELLA

No, thank you! I've got a quest to get back to!

SNOW WHITE

Good luck, Cinderella. I hope you find what you're looking for.

PRINCESSES

Goodbye Cinderella! Take care! Good luck! Etc.

                CINDERELLA exits. PRINCESSES sit and
                play cards. LIGHTS: BLACKOUT.

SCENE SIX

LIGHTS: RISE dimly on cave. Lots of fog. CINDERELLA,
    PRINCE, TOUCHSTONE, and MIRROR enter.

MIRROR
We made it. The Cavern of the Crystal Pump!

TOUCHSTONE
How do you know this is the right cave?

MIRROR
There's a sign over there that says "Welcome to The Cavern
of the Crystal Pump".

THEY look and sure enough, there's the
sign.

ALL
Oh yeah! Look at that! There is a sign! Etc!

TOUCHSTONE
This place is really spooky!

PRINCE
You can say that again.

TOUCHSTONE
This place is really spooky!

PRINCE
How did I know you were going to say that?

TOUCHSTONE
That's me. A reliable source of comic schtick! Would you
like to see me slip on a banana peel?

ALL

NO!!!

CINDERELLA

What's that over there?

> SHE crosses to a wall and takes a parchment
> from it and blows off the dust.

PRINCE

What is it?

CINDERELLA

It looks like a riddle.
        (Reads.)
I run over fields and woods all day.
Under the bed at night, I sit alone.
My tongue hangs out, up and to the rear,
Waiting to be filled in the morning.
What am I?

> LIGHTS: RISE to reveal letters on the floor.

MIRROR

What's that all about?

> COLONEL KLAMAUK, KLINK and
> KLANK enter with swords.

COLONEL KLAMAUK

Ich werde Ihnen sagen, worum es geht!   (I'll tell you what
it's about!)

> THEY look at EACH OTHER, confused.

PRINCE

I'm sorry. We don't speak whatever language that is you're
speaking.

MIRROR

That's not exactly true.

PRINCE

Mirror?

MIRROR

Along with being very articulate and quite well read, I'm also fluent in over 30 languages.

TOUCHSTONE

You never told us that!

MIRROR

You never asked.

PRINCE

What is he saying then?

MIRROR

He said, "I'll tell you what it's about!"

COLONEL KLAMAUK

Sie müssen das Rätsel um Rechtschreibung aus der Antwort auf den Boden zu beantworten. Eine falsche Bewegung und du bist tot!   (You must answer the riddle by spelling out the answer on the floor. One wrong move and you are a goner! Bwah-ha-ha-ha-ha!)

MIRROR

"You must answer the riddle by spelling out the answer on the floor. One wrong move and you are a goner! Bwah-ha-ha-ha-ha!"

PRINCE

What do they want?

MIRROR

Was wollen Sie?   (What do you want?)

COLONEL KLAMAUK

Was denkst du wir wollen, Dummkopf? (What do you think we want, you fool?)

MIRROR

What do you think we want, you fool?

PRINCE

Mirror!

MIRROR

Sorry.

COLONEL KLAMAUK

Wir wollen die Crystal Pumps!   (We want the Crystal Pumps!)

MIRROR

They want the Crystal Pumps!

PRINCE

That part we understood. But why?

MIRROR

Warum?   (Why?)

COLONEL KLAMAUK

Es ist für unser furchtloser Anführer. Er will deinen Crystal Pumps für sich. (It's for our fearless leader. He wants the Crystal Pump for himself.)

KLINK

Yeah! Er mag in Frauenkleidern zu kleiden. (Yeah! He likes to dress in women's clothing.)

KLANK

Und singt Broadway Melodien! (And sing showtunes!)

MIRROR

They said it's for their fearless leader. He likes to dress in women's clothing and sing showtunes.

CINDERELLA

That's very weird.

COLONEL KLAMAUK

Lesen Sie die Rätsel wieder!   (Read the riddle again!)

MIRROR

He wants you to read the riddle again.

CINDERELLA

 I run over fields and woods all day.
Under the bed at night, I sit alone.
My tongue hangs out, up and to the rear,
Waiting to be filled in the morning.
What am I?

Colonel Klamauk

Hmmmmmm.

TOUCHSTONE

What could it mean?

CINDERELLA

Shoes!

PRINCE

Shoes?

TOUCHSTONE

Shoes?

60

MIRROR

Shoes?

COLONEL KLAMAUK

Shoes?

KLINK

Shoes?

KLANK

Shoes?

COLONEL KLAMAUK
Of course…the letter "S"!

> HE steps on the letter "S". There is a
> rumbling. THREE GIANT SPIDERS enter
> and drag HIM off screaming.
> KLINK and KLANK run off screaming.

CINDERELLA
Only the riddle is written in ancient Hebrew, and everybody
knows that in ancient Hebrew the word for shoe begins with
an "N".

PRINCE
You can read ancient Hebrew?

CINDERELLA
Of course. Can't you? My father taught me.

PRINCE
Impressive.

OLD PROFESSOR
(From offstage.)
I agree. It is impressive. You have learned your lessons well!

                              HE enters. Very old and grey. Wearing a
                              fedora and a leather jacket.

                              CINDERELLA
Father?

                              OLD PROFESSOR
It's me, Cinderella.

                              CINDERELLA
When you didn't come back, we assumed you'd been killed.

                              OLD PROFESSOR
Dead? No. Just trapped in this cave by those giant spiders.

                              CINDERELLA
How did you survive all this time?

                              OLD PROFESSOR
Dried kumquats.

                              CINDERELLA
What's a kumquat?

                              OLD PROFESSOR
A kumquat is a subtropical, pulpy, citrus fruit, used chiefly
for preserves.

                              CINDERELLA
I never knew that.

                              MIRROR
I did.

                              OLD PROFESSOR
I always pack my pockets full of them when I'm on a quest.
Would you like some?

CINDERELLA
Uh…no. I ate before I left.

OLD PROFESSOR
Cinderella. I've got to know. Your stepmother…is she still
the same sweet, lovable girl I left behind?

CINDERELLA
No, Father…she's been sort of…grumpy since you
disappeared to tell you the truth.

OLD PROFESSOR
I can't wait to see her again. That is, if we ever get out of
here.

CINDERELLA
We'll get out of here together, Father.

OLD PROFESSOR
How will we? We can't go back. Only forwards.

CINDERELLA
That's all right. I'm not leaving without the Crystal Pumps.

OLD PROFESSOR
Like father, like daughter. But if we're going to do this,
Cinderella, then let's do it right.
          (Pulls out a fedora.)
Welcome to the family business.

          HE places the fedora on HER head.
          MUSIC: Adventure music plays.
          There are a series of small scenes depicting
          the GROUP tip toeing across the floor.
          Running from SPIDERS. Taking a dance
          break, running, ducking, and covering.

Finally removing, slowly, the CRYSTAL
PUMPS from a pedestal and replacing with
a television. THEY look around. Nothing.
THEY smile and congratulate EACH
OTHER. Then there is smoke and
SPIDERS. THEY all run helter skelter in all
directions. LIGHTS: BLACKOUT.

SCENE SEVEN

LIGHTS: Rise on Cinderella's cottage. STEPMOTHER,
           BRUMHILDA and GRIZELDA are tied up.
           CINDERELLA enters.

CINDERELLA
Stepmother? What happened?

SHE unties THEM.

STEPMOTHER
It was Cinderella…not you…the other Cinderella…she's evil.
At first we thought she was you…

BRUMHILDA
But then she was all like "Do this!" and "Do that!"

STEPMOTHER
Feed the fish!

BRUMHILDA
Milk the cow!

GRIZELDA
Mow the grass!

STEPMOTHER
Beat the rugs!

BRUMHILDA
Take out the trash!

STEPMOTHER
Churn the buttermilk! Oh, how I hate buttermilk!

ALL
Buttermilk!!!

THEY start bawling.

CINDERELLA
Stepmother. I found someone. I think you might know him.

OLD PROFESSOR enters.

STEPMOTHER
Henry? Is that you?

OLD PROFESSOR
It's me…and stop calling me that.

STEPMOTHER
Where have you been all this time?

OLD PROFESSOR
Trapped in the Cavern of the Crystal Pump by a bunch of giant, man-eating spiders.

STEPMOTHER
How did you keep from going mad?

OLD PROFESSOR
I did what any man would do in that situation. I tried on women's shoes.

STEPMOTHER
You poor thing!

OLD PROFESSOR
I'll never understand how you women can walk in those blasted things!

STEPMOTHER
Oh, Henry!

OLD PROFESSOR
I told you to stop calling me Henry!

STEPMOTHER
But that's your name.

OLD PROFESSOR
I prefer to be called…"Indiana"!

STEPMOTHER
But honey, we named the dog Indiana!!!

ALL laugh.

CINDERELLA
Where did Clockwork Cindy go?

BRUMHILDA
She went to the ball!

GRIZELDA
She left with some pointy eared midget!

CINDERELLA
Dr. Thingamahoochie!

ALL
THINGAMABOB!!!

CINDERELLA
Whatever.

STEPMOTHER
They're up to no good Cinderella! They were talking about
overthrowing the King and Queen and ruling the kingdom!

CINDERELLA
This is all my fault.

BRUMHILDA

So? Are we going to the ball or not?

GRIZELDA

Yeah? We're not going to let Clockwork Cindy get away with this, are we?

CINDERELLA

No. We're not! I've got the Crystal Pumps and nothing is going to keep me from going to the ball!

LIGHTS: BLACKOUT.

SCENE EIGHT

LIGHTS: RISE on palace. The KING and QUEEN are tied
         up. DR. THINGAMABOB and CLOCKWORK
         CINDY wear THEIR crowns. DR.
         THINGAMABOB'S is way too big and keeps
         falling down. ALL wear masquerade masks.

DR. THINGAMABOB
Well-well-well! Who ever knew taking over the kingdom
would be so easy!

CLOCKWORK CINDY
Ho-Ho-Ho!

DR. THINGAMABOB
Remind me to adjust your vocal mechanism later.

CLOCKWORK CINDY
Ho-Ho-Ho!

DR. THINGAMABOB
That's right, baby! And there's nobody who can stop us!
Bwah-ha-ha-ha-ha!

CINDERELLA enters.

CINDERELLA
Not so fast Dr. Thingamadoodle!

DR. THINGAMABOB
Thingamabob!

CINDERELLA
Whatever.

DR. THINGAMABOB
Cinderella?

CLOCKWORK CINDY
Ho-Ho-Ho?

CINDERELLA
Thought you could just waltz into the ball and take over the kingdom, huh?

DR. THINGAMABOB
Something like that.

CINDERELLA
Well, you thought wrong. Surrender!

DR. THINGAMABOB
Or what? You'll bake me a pie? Clockwork Cindy! Attack!

> THEY remove shoes and battle. Evenly matched. Just when it seems CINDERELLA is finished, the PRINCE enters, wearing a mask. HE fights CLOCKWORK CINDY.

DR. THINGAMABOB
Who is that?

> TOUCHSTONE and MIRROR have entered and are trying to free the KING and QUEEN.

TOUCHSTONE AND MIRROR
It's Prince Charming!

KING AND QUEEN
Prince Charming?

DR. THINGAMABOB
Prince Charming?

CINDERELLA

Prince Charming?

CLOCKWORK CINDY

Ho-Ho-Ho?

PRINCE

That's right!
(Hands CINDERELLA HER sword.)
Here's your sword, Cinderella.

CINDERELLA

You know my name? How?

PRINCE

Everybody knows the daughter of the world's most famous
explorer! Nice shoes by the way!

CINDERELLA

Thanks!

THEY continue to fight until the BAD
GUYS are vanquished.

QUEEN

Oh Charlie! We are so proud of you!

KING

Yes, Son! Very heroic! I think there might be a song in your
future!

PRINCE

Thank you.

KING

And who is this young lady?

CINDERELLA
My name is…
            (Clock strikes twelve.)
Oh no! Midnight! My time is up!

            SHE starts to run out.

PRINCE
Wait, Cinderella. I need to tell you something.

CINDERELLA
I can't stay. Please. It's not you. It's me.

            ALL groan.

CINDERELLA
I think you are a very nice guy and a pretty good swordsman
and all, but you see, I'm in love with someone else.

PRINCE
What?

CINDERELLA
I wanted to come here and meet you, but along the way I met
another guy. I need to go find him and tell him how I feel.

PRINCE
I see. Do what you must, but don't forget these.

            HE hands HER the CRYSTAL PUMPS.

CINDERELLA
Thank you.

PRINCE
And don't forget this.

                    HE places the fedora on HER head.

                        CINDERELLA
How did you…?
                    (HE removes mask.)
Charlie? Why did….I didn't…I…Hi. My name is Cinderella.
Pleased to meet you.

                        THEY kiss.

                        CINDERELLA
Your name is Charlie?

                        PRINCE
Yep.

                        CINDERELLA
Charlie Charming?

                        PRINCE
Yep. Interested in becoming Mrs. Charlie Charming?

                        CINDERELLA
I think I might keep my maiden name.

                        PRINCE
What's that?

                        CINDERELLA
Jones.

                    SHE winks at the audience. MIRROR
                    comes forward.

                        MIRROR
And so, with peace restored to the kingdom…

FAIRY GODPERSON
(Offstage.)

Wait!

HE enters with HIS usual flourish.

CINDERELLA

It's my Fairy Godperson!

FAIRY GODPERSON

You are not narrating this show, Magic Mirror.

MIRROR

Sorry.

FAIRY GODPERSON

In fact, I think your narrating days are behind you. Magic
Mirror on the wall, what's your fondest wish of all?

MIRROR

Well...I'd like to be a real girl.

FAIRY GODPERSON

Very well. Bippity-boppity...oh, to heck with it! Come on
out from behind the wall.

MIRROR comes out.

MIRROR

I'm a real girl! I'm a real girl!

TOUCHSTONE

Ok, Pinocchio...here...
(Hands HER a handkerchief.)
Wipe your face off. What about me Fairy Whatever? Do I get
a wish?

FAIRY GODPERSON
Of course, dear Touchstone. What do you desire most?

TOUCHSTONE
Uh..........

MIRROR
Now he's speechless.

FAIRY GODPERSON
How about your very own HBO Comedy Special?

TOUCHSTONE
Uh..........

FAIRY GODPERSON
You're welcome. My good King and Queen?

KING and QUEEN look at EACH OTHER.

KING and QUEEN
Grandchildren!

EVERYONE looks at PRINCE and
CINDERELLA.

FAIRY GODPERSON
Uh...I'll get back to you on that one.
(Changes subject.)
What about you, Cinderella? What is your heart's fondest
desire?

CINDERELLA
My wish already came true.

SHE dips the PRINCE and kisses HIM.

FAIRY GODPERSON
And of course, they all lived happily ever after. Now, is this a party or what? Music please!

MUSIC: Something festive. EVERYBODY gets down with THEIR bad selves.

THE END

Thank you for purchasing and reading this play. If you enjoyed it, we'd appreciate a review on Amazon.com.

On the following pages you will find a selection of other plays from the Black Box Theatre Publishing Company catalog presented for you at no additional cost.

Enjoy!!!

www.blackboxtheatrepublishing.com

NOW AVAILABLE!!!

"Poop Happens!" in this family friendly cowboy comedy!

So, Who Was That Masked Guy Anyway? is the story of Ernie, the grandson of the original Masked Cowboy, a lawman who fought for truth, justice and the cowboy way in the old west. Now that Grandpa is getting on in years he's looking for someone to carry on for him. The only problem? Ernie doesn't know anything about being a cowboy. He's never seen a real cow, he's allergic to milk and to tell the truth he doesn't know one end of a horse from another...but beware, before it's all over, the poop is sure to hit the fans!

Cast Size: 21 Flexible M-F Roles Doubling Possible.

Royalties: $50.00 per performance.

Running Time: Approximately 90 minutes.

NOW AVAILABLE!!!

WANTED: SANTA CLAUS is the story of what happens
when a group of department store moguls decide to replace
Santa Claus with the shiny new "KRINGLE 3000",
codenamed...ROBO-SANTA! Now it's up to Santa's elves to
save the day! But Santa's in no shape to take on his stainless
steel counterpart! He'll have to train for his big comeback.
Enter Mickey, one of the toughest elves of all time! He'll get
Santa ready for the big showdown! But it's going to mean
reaching deep down inside to find "the eye of the reindeer"!

Cast Size 23 Flexible M-F Roles Doubling Possible.

Royalties: $50.00 per performance.

Running Time: Approximately 90 Minutes.

NOW AVAILABLE!!!

At the edge of the universe sits The Long John Cafe. A
place where the average guy and the average "Super" guy
can sit and have a cup of coffee and just be themselves...or,
someone else if that's what they want. The cafe is populated
by iconic figures of the 20th Century, including cowboys,
hippies, super heroes and movie stars. They've come to
celebrate the end of the old Century and the beginning of
tomorrow! That is, if they make it through the night! It
seems the evil Dr. McNastiman has other plans for our
heroes. Like their total destruction!

Cast Size: 17 9M 8F.

Royalties: $50.00 per performance.

Running Time: Approximately 90 Minutes.

NOW AVAILABLE!!!

Jacklyn Sparrow and the Lady Pirates of the Caribbean is our brand new swashbuckling pirate parody complete with bloodthirsty buccaneers in massive sword clanking battle scenes!! A giant wise cracking parrot named Polly!! Crazy obsessions with eye liner!! And just who is Robert, the Dreaded Phylum Porifera!!!

Please Note: We offer large and small cast versions of this play. Cast and royalty numbers for both are below.

Cast Size: 45/13 Flexible M-F Roles Doubling Possible.

Royalties: $50.00 per performance.

Running Time: Approximately120/45 Minutes.

NOW AVAILABLE!!!

"May the Dwarf be with you in this wacky take on the classic fairy tale which will have audiences rolling in the floor with laughter!

What happens when you mix an articulate mirror, a conceited queen, a prince dressed in purple, seven little people with personality issues, a basket of kumquats and a little Star Wars for good measure?

Cast Size: 12 Flexible M-F Roles.

Royalty: $50.00 per performance.

Running Time: Approximately 45 Minutes.

NOW AVAILABLE!!!

Dear John

An ode to the potty.

"My dreams of thee flow softly.
They enter with tender rush.
The still soft sound which echoes,
When I lower the lid and flush."

They say that porcelain is the best antenna for creativity. At least that's what this cast of young people believe in Dear John: An ode to the potty! The action of this one act play takes place almost entirely behind the doors of five bathroom stalls. This short comedy is dedicated to all those term papers, funny pages and Charles Dickens' novels that have been read behind closed (stall) doors!

Cast Size: 10 5M 5F.

Royalties: $35.00 per performance.

Running Time: Approximately 15 Minutes.

NOW AVAILABLE!!!

Declassified after 40 years!

On December 21, 1970, an impromptu meeting took place between the King of Rock and Roll and the Leader of the Free World.

Elvis Meets Nixon (Operation Wiggle) is a short comedy which offers one possible (and ultimately ridiculous) explanation of what happened during that meeting.

Cast Size: 2 M with 1 Offstage F Voice.

Royalties: $35.00 per performance.

Running Time: Approximately 10 Minutes.

NOW AVAILABLE!!!

In the beginning, there was a man.
Then there was a woman.
And then there was this piece of fruit...
...and that's when everything went horribly wrong!
Even Adam is a short comedy exploring the relationship
between men and women right from day one.

Why doesn't he ever bring her flowers like he used to?
Why doesn't she laugh at his jokes anymore?
And just who is that guy in the red suit?
And how did she convince him to eat that fruit, anyway?

Cast Size: 3 2M-1F.

Royalties: $35.00 per performance.

Running Time: Approximately 10 Minutes.

NOW AVAILABLE!!!

Count Dracula is bored. He's pretty much sucked
Transylvania dry, and he's looking for a new challenge. So
it's off to New York, New York! The Big Apple! The town
that never sleeps...that'll pose a challenge for sure.
Dracula purchases The Carfax Theatre and decides to put on
a big, flashy Broadway show!

Cast Size: 50 Flexible M/F roles with Doubling Possible.

Royalties: $50.00 per performance.

Running Time: Approximately 90 Minutes.

NOW AVAILABLE!!!

THE FOUR PRESIDENTS is an educational play which examines the lives and characters of four of the most colorful personalities to hold the office. George Washington, Abraham Lincoln, Theodore Roosevelt and Richard Nixon. Much of the dialogue comes from the Presidents' own words.

A perfect show for schools!

Cast Size: 10 Flexible M-F Roles with Doubling Possible.

Royalties: $50.00 per performance.

Running Time: Approximately 60 Minutes.

NOW AVAILABLE!!!

The lights rise on a beautiful sunset.
A mermaid is silhouetted against an ocean backdrop.
Hauntingly familiar music fills the air.
Then...the Lawyer shows up.
And that's when the fun really begins!

It's The Little Mermaid (More or Less.)

Cast Size: 30 Flexible M-F Roles with Doubling Possible.

Royalties: $50.00 per performance.

Running Time: Approximately 45 Minutes.

NOW AVAILABLE!!!

Cinderella and the Quest for the Crystal Pump, is the story of a young girl seeking a life beyond the endless chores heaped upon her by her grouchy stepmother and two stepsisters. But more than anything, Cinderella wants to go to the prince's masquerade ball, but there's one problem...she has nothing to wear! Luckily, her Fairy Godperson has a few ideas.

Please Note: This play is available in large and small cast versions. Both cast sizes and royalty rates are listed below.

Cast Size: 30/13 Flexible M-F Roles with Some Doubling Possible.

Royalties: $50.00 per performance.

Running Time: Approximately 90/45 Minutes.

NOW AVAILABLE!!!

Shorespeare is loosely based on a Midsummer Night's Dream.
Shakespeare, with the help of Cupid, has landed at the Jersey Shore.
Cupid inspires him to write a play about two New Jersey
sweethearts, Cleo and Toni. Shakespeare is put off by their accent
and way of talking, but decides to send the two teenagers on a
course of true love. Toni and Cleo are determined to get married
right after they graduate from high school, but in order to do so they
must pass this course of true love that Cupid's pixies create and
manipulate. As they travel along the boardwalk at the Jersey Shore,
Cleo and Toni, meet a handful of historical figures disguised as the
carnies. Confucius teaches Cleo the "Zen of Snoring", Charles
Ponzi teaches them the importance of "White Lies", Leonardo Da
Vinci shows them the "Art of Multitasking", and finally they meet
Napolean who tries to help them to "Accept Shortcomings" of each
other. After going through all these lessons, the sweethearts decide
that marriage should wait, and Cupid is proud of Shakespeare who
has finally reached out to the modern youth.

NOW AVAILABLE!!!

Everyone has heard the phrase, "it's the squeaky wheel that gets the oil," but how many people know the Back-story? The story begins in a kingdom far, far away over the rainbow – a kingdom called Spokend. This kingdom of wheels is a happy one for the gods have blessed the tiny hamlet with plentiful sunshine, water and most important –oil. Until a terrible drought starts to dry up all the oil supplies. What is to be done?

The powerful barons of industry and politicians decide to hold a meeting to decide how to solve the situation. Since Spokend is a democracy all the citizens come to the meeting but their voices are ignored – especially the voice of one of the poorer citizens of the community suffering from a squeak that can only be cured with oil, Spare Wheel and his wife Fifth Wheel. Despite Spare Wheel's desperate pleas for oil, he is ignored and sent home without any help or consideration.

Without oil, Spare Wheel's squeak becomes so bad he loses his job and his family starts to suffer when his sick leave and unemployment benefits run out. What is he to do? Spare Wheel and Fifth Wheel develop a scheme that uses the squeak to their advantage against the town magistrate Big Wheel who finally relents and gives over the oil. Thus, for years after in the town of Spokend citizens in need of help are told "It's the squeaky wheel that gets the oil."

NOW AVAILABLE!!!

Once upon a time, a beautiful princess was placed
under a magic spell by an evil fairy. A spell that
would cause her to fall into a deep, deep sleep. A
sleep from which she would awaken 1000 years
later.
It's "Sleeping Beauty meets Buck Rogers" in this
play for young audiences.

Royalties: $50.00 per performance.

Cast Size: 13 with flexible extras.

Running Time: Approximately 45 minutes.

NOW AVAILABLE!!!

Santa Claus. Frosty. Rudolph. Jack Frost.

This Christmas…if you've got a problem and if you can find them then maybe you can hire…THE SLEIGH TEAM!!!

The team is hired by lowly clerk, Bob Crachit to help his boss, the miserly old Ebenezer Scrooge find a little "Christmas Spirit"!

Royalties: $50.00 per performance.

Cast Size: 6

Running Time: Approximately 45 minutes.

NOW AVAILABLE!!!

The Odd Princesses is a parody/mash-up that opens with a group of princesses assembled for a card game in the palace of the notoriously messy Snow White. Late to arrive to the party is the perpetually neat Cinderella who has run away from home after becoming fed up with being treated like a maid by her stepmother. With no where else to turn, the two total opposites decide to move in together! What could go wrong?

Royalties: $50.00 per performance.

Cast Size: 8 with extras possible.

Running Time: Approximately 45 minutes.

NOW AVAILABLE!!!

Eager to escape the clutches of the Big Bad Wolf once and for all, the Three Little Pigs build a time machine and travel back in time 150 million years to the Jurassic era where they quickly discover they have problems much bigger than the Big Bad Wolf. Much, much, much bigger!!!

Royalties $35.00 per performance.

Cast Size: 6+ extras with flexible M-F roles.

Running Time: Approximately 30 minutes.

NOW AVAILABLE!!!

Dr. Victor "Vickie" Frankenstein has just inherited his grandfather's castle in foggy Transylvania...but what secrets lie in the ultra-secret, sub-terrainian laboratory located beneath the castle??? It's a little bit monster story and a little bit Rock and Roll!

Royalties $50.00 per performance.

Cast Size: 16. 8 principle roles, 8+ Extras possible.

Running Time: Approximately one hour.